TALES OF KRISHNA

ANILA BHAVANARI

Made with ❤ on the Notion Press Platform
www.notionpress.com

This little pages belongs to my soul as i was a Radha Krishna devote.

Contents

Preface

Krishna, the word itself says the meaning of attractive.
    Who took their eyes from him? Any body?
    Who taught us like him?
    Who plays music like Krishna?
    Who punish us for our mistakes?
    Who attracts everyone as he do?
    Who help us in everything?
    No one would be like him....

Foreword

Can i forword this book to the person who was very fond in Krishna stories?

Yes, this was for you.

Acknowledgements

"I want to thank all the people out there who were trying their best to bring our mythology back."

Authors Voice.

As we all know, there are many things and many stories about Krishna. These are just a short stories and these are about some of the people in Krishna's life..

He taught us everything by Bhagavadgita. He sacrificed a lot for his people. He put his efforts in every work he does, for the sake of his people.

As i was very fond of Krishna...

Writing his stories made my smile most beautiful...

Note.

These are just stories of Krishna as authors knowledge. This book was written based on purana stories.

CHAPTER ONE

RUKMINI.

Rukmini was the first wife in Ashtabharyas.

Her love towards Krishna was immortal.

She was the daughter of Bhismak who was the king of Vidarbha. Rukmini had a brother Rukmi. One day Rukmi told his father and sister that he was interested to her sisters marriage with Shishupala the king of chedi. By hearing this Naradha came onto earth and told Bhismak about Krishna and his powers. The king and Rukmini heard his stories with great of interest and Bhismak decided to marry her daughter to Krishna. But Rukmi went on opposite to this and decided Rukmini's marriage with Shishupala. Rukmini decided to elope with Krishna against her brother without knowing him. She sent a letter to Krishna with her loyal person saying that to take her with him from this reluctant marriage. She also said that she din't accept anyone as her husband except Sri Krishna. By seeing this Krishna decided to go near Rukmini to bring her with him.

As the whole area of Vidarbha was decorated with full of flowers and emerged with people who are busy on their works for marriage. Rukmini was waiting was Krishna to take her away with him. She was in worry and also in a great faithful mood that Krishna will definitely comes near her.

As all were going on hurry, Rukmini went to Ambikadevi temple to make her wish fulfill among with many soldiers. There she prayed goddess to send Krishna near her.

As she was going back from the temple. Krishna came near her, and infront of many soldiers Krishna and Balarama eloped with Rukmini with her. By listening this Rukmi went on angry and decided to kill Krishna and get back her sister. Many kings who attend to marriage stepped back to fought with Krishna. Rukmi himself went on near Krishna. He went near Krishna and tried to kill him but Krishna defeated him. And when Krishna tried to kill him. Rukmini pleased Krishna to leave her brother without killing. So Krishna decided to leave Rukmi and made his head shaved as symbol of defeat.

Krishna brought Rukmini to Dwarka. The people were happy for their marriage as Rukmini.

CHAPTER TWO

JAMBAVATI, SATYABHAMA.

Jambavati was the second wife and Satyabhama was the third wife of Krishna among ashtabharyas.

Syamantaka mani was owned by Satrajit the yadava king. Once Krishna asked Satrajit to give syamantaka mani to him as he was very found of it. But Satrajit refused to give it and told him that it was the jewel presented by Surya deva who he worshipped.

One day Satrajit's brother Prasena went on to forest to hunt animals by wearing syamantaka jewel. On his way he was killed by lion. Jambavan who went on to that direction seen syamantaka mani and gifted it to his daughter to play.

As the king Satrajit felt sad about his brothers death and also realized about the missing Syamantaka mani. He put his words on Krishna that he had stolen it. Krishna felt sad, thought to find it and on to search for it. He went on to the forest direction that Prasena went to and found Jambavan's place with Syamantaka mani. Krishna asked him to give it back but Jambavan refused it and called him to war if he want it.

As they fought for many days then jambavan realised that Krishna was an avatar of Rama and surrendered himself to Krishna by giving Syamantaka mani and his daughter Jambavati to him.

When Krishna went on to his kingdom with Syamantakamani, he told Satrajit the story behind the missing of Syamantaka mani. Then Satrajit pleased Krishna to forgive him. And he also married his daughter Satyabhama who was a great warrior and also the incarnation of Bhudevi.

CHAPTER THREE

KALINDI.

Kalindi was fourth wife of Krishna among Ashtabharyas.

When Sri Krishna was born in jail. Vasudeva decided to take him to Vrindavan to place Krishna near Nanda and Yashoda. At the middle of his way, he requested river Yamuna to make a way to him to cross the river. Kind Yamuna helped Vasudev to cross her. When Vasudev was carrying Krishna on his head, Yamuna touched Krishna's feet and she went on calm herself. She was impressed by his touch and had fallen in love with Krishna. As Krishna grown near the Yamuna river from his childhood. Kalindi loved to see him always.

One day Krishna killed Kaliya who was king of snakes for polluting Yamuna river. Vrindavan people caught to diseases by drinking water of Yamuna which was polluted by Kaliya. So Krishna decided to kill Kaliya. Yamuna was again impressed by Krishna's behaviour and fallen in love with Krishna. And she decided to marry him.

When Pandavas built Indraprasthanam as their home near Yamuna river. Krishna decided to meet them. As he went on near Pandavas, Yudhisthira told Krishna to stay with them for one day. Krishna too accepted it and stayed with them.

At the evening when the Krishna and Arjuna went to near Yamuna. They both saw a beautiful girl who was in penance. Krishna who fell in love with her beauty told Arjuna to seek her information. Then Kalindi told Arjuna that she was daughter of Surya dev and Sanjana and also she was in penance to marry lord Vishnu. Arjuna told Krishna what Kalindi told him. Then Krishna went on to Kalindi and said that he was the eight avatar of lord Vishnu. Then they both decided to marry.

Krishna took Kalindi to Dwarka the next day. There they married each other with all the blessings.

mi. And there they both married formally in front of many people with their blessings.

CHAPTER FOUR

MITHRAVINDA.

Mithravinda was the fifth wife of Krishna among Ashtabharya.

Mithravinda was daughter of Jayasena from Avanti. A biggest swayamvara was arranged to Mithravinda by her brothers Vindya and Anuvindya. Many messages were sent to all the kings to attend the Mithravinda swayamvara.

Balaram sent Krishna to Swayamvara even tough they din't get any message from Jaya sena. He also told that they were grouped with many kindoms and was going on with huge empire. He said Krishna to marry Mithravinda so that they can be their side after their marriage. Krishna took his sister Subhadra with him to know Mithravinda words about their marriage.

When Krishna too attended the Swayamvara with all the kings. Then Mithravinda chooses Krishna to marry him. But Vindya, Anuvindya who are friends of Kauravas got opposed to her sisters decision and decided to kill him. Then Krishna defeated all of them to marrya Mithravinda. Then Krishna told his sister to ask Mithravinda as she was ready to marry Krishna. When Subhadra came out and told Krishna about Mithravinda acceptance on their marriage. They both took Mithravinda to Dwaraka.

There they married with all the blessings.

CHAPTER FIVE

NAGNAJITI.

Nagnajiti was sixth wife of Krishna among Ashtabharya.

She was also the incarnation of Nila devi. She was also called Satya.

Nagnajiti was the daughter of Nagnajita who was the ruler of kosala. Nagnajita was the brother of Yashoda mother of Krishna. He was the great king who respects and treats people as their own children.

As the days passed Nagnajita arranged swayamvara to their daughter Nagnajit.

Many members attended to marry Nagnajiti. On swayamvara Nagnajita put a condition during the process. He told that who won the competition can marry Nagnajiti without any doubt.

The condition was complicated some, it was they have to defeat seven bulls that belongs to king. As the first kings thought they can defeat them on a single hand but the action happened their was entirely reverse. As the turn of every king had completed, no one defeated them.

By listening these Krishna came from Dwaraka to swayamvara to attend it.

By listening the Krishna's Arrival Nagnajita went on to welcome him to the Swayamvara. Then Krishna told about his desire to marry Nagnajiti.

Nagnajiti told Krishna if he defeat his bulls then he can marry Nagnajiti. Krishna accepted his request and went on to defeat them. There he transformed himself into five parts and defeated all of them.

Then Nagnajiti got impressed by Krishna.

They both came to Dwaraka and got married by all the blessings.

CHAPTER SIX

BADHRA.

Bhadra was the seventh wife of Krishna among Ashtabharyas.

Bhadra was the daughter of Dhrishtaketu and Shrutakirti. She decided to marry Krishna in first sight on swayamvara. His brother was very fond on Krishna and happily agreed her sister marriage with him. As his father agreed to her marriage. Krishna took Bhadra to Dwaraka.

Their they married with all their blessings.

CHAPTER SEVEN

LAKSHMANA.

Lakshmana was the eighth wife of Krishna among Ashtabharyas.

She was also known as Madra.

Lakshmana's father put an archery competition to the kings who came their to marry his daughter. All the kings including Duryodhana from Hastinapur came for Swayamvara. But no one won the competition. Arjuna who was the king on archery had also missed the goal. But Krishna took the goal and won it. Lakshmana agreed Krishna as her husband. They both went on to Dwaraka.

They married each other with all the blessings.

CHAPTER EIGHT

HANUMAN.

When lord Ram gave a boon to Hanuman that he will live as chiranjeeva after the war with Ravana.

Hanuman in Dwapara yuga was waiting for his lord to appear near him in himalaya mountains.

One day Narada went near Krishna and Rukmini and told them that Hanuman was waiting to them in himalayas. As Krishna learned about Hanuman he was very happy about his waiting.

As the days passed Krishna went near Hanuman on Ramanavami as Hanuman performing a puja for him. Krishna went near him and appear near Hanuman. Hanuman got much happy for seeing his lord again.

When pandavas were in agnatavasam. Bhima did penance to Hanuman to give him much strength to fight against Kauravas. As Bhima's wish

Hanuman had given much strength to Bhima and helped him in Kurukshetra race.

CHAPTER NINE

16,000 WIVES.

Narakasura a demon from pragjyotisha kingdom. Who made all the women as his slaves and put them on jail in his own kingdom. As Satyabhama learned this from her friend. She goes near Krishna and tells him about the demon Narakasura. On the other way Narakasura took a boon from Brahma as he was only killed by his mother not by anyone from the world. Brahma granted it.

He occupied all the territories from the world and made many women as slaves. After listening Satyabhama words Krishna told her to get ready for the war to kill him. Braved Satyabhama fought the war to help all the people. When the war was going on, Krishna told Narakasura and Satyabhama relation as they were mother and son. Narakasura stunned by knowing the fact and asked Satyabhama a wish. Satyabhama who was the mother of his waited to grant him whatever he want. Then Narakasura asked Krishna to celebrate his birthday as Narakasura vada and Dewali. Krishna and Satyabhama accepted his request and told him that all can celebrate your death as a big festival.

And Krishna released all the women from Narakasura. Then they told him that they are not ready to go to their homes because no one accept them as they stayed many days near Narakasura. So Krishna himself divided as 16,000 forms and made all them as his wives.

CHAPTER TEN

SAMBA

Samba was son of lord Krishna.

As Krishna had Astabharya Every one was happy with their children. But

Jambavathi was not blessed with any children and she was upset with it. One day she asked Krishna that she want a baby boy. So Krishna went to forest and prayed Shiva to grant him with a baby boy. So Shiva appeared in Arthanariswara form and blessed Krishna and Jambavathi will become parents for a baby child. As Samba was the other name of Shiva, Krishna and Jambavathi named this Boy as Samba.

Later after the birth of Samba they both given birth to other children. As Samba was playing with their friends on outside near Pindraka. One day the sages Vishwamitra, Asita, Kanva, Durvasa, Bhirgu, Angiras, Vamadevi, Atri, Vashishta, Kashyapa and the others visited Dwaraka to look Krishna. And then they went to a holy place called Pindraka. There Samba decided to make a prank thing on the sages with his friends. So he dressed up like a pregnant women and went near sages and asked them whether this women gives birth to boy or girl. Then Narada got angry and cursed Samba saying that he will give birth to a iron rod. When all the friends uncovered his belly they seen an iron rod stick in it. All they got fear and they went to Ugrasena. After listening all the story, Ugrasena took iron rod from Samba belly and thrown it into the sea. Then iron rod got into pieces. The one piece of iron rod was swallowed by a fish in the sea. Jara a fisher man took that fish from the sea to eat. While cutting the fish he seen a small piece of iron rod. So he tied it to his arrow end.

And after the mahabharatha war, Gandhari curse Krishna as his yadava dynasty will destroy. So after the curse Krishna observed that, the people in his dynasty were addicted to alcohol and they were fighting among themselves. Krishna thought it would be the end of his Dynasty and went near Arjuna saying that to save their women. And he went near a tree, went on thinking about their people. This jara who was a fisher man came there with his arrow to hunt animals. He mistook Krishna feet as deer and leaved his arrow to the Krishna feet. After that he pleased Krishna. Krishna who knows that it was his fate consoled Jara. Then he departed from his body and went to Vaikunta.

CHAPTER ELEVEN

SRIDAMA.

When Krishna and Radha were in golok and living with gopis with their happy life.

Sridama how was a great devote to Sri Krishna went near him with a message from Brahma. As he was Krishna's devote, he saw the people in golok were very fond of Radha who was the symbol of pure love. Then this Sridama got angry on Radha and her people to not praising his lord.

One day Radha got angry on Krishna because she heard from a friend that Krishna was very fond on gopis and went on dance with them last night. So she decided to yell on Krishna about this issue. When Krishna came near Radha with Sridama. Radha got angry with the incident and yelled at Krishna. As Sridama was a great devote his anger filled on her and cursed her that she will leave Krishna for 100 years and will go to earth leaving him. Then Radha got anger and she too curse Sridama that he will born as demon in his next life.

CHAPTER TWELVE

MIRABAI.

Mirabai was a grand daughter of Rao Dudaji king of Rathod Dynasty, Rajasthan.

Ratna singh and Virkvari were her parents. As her parents died early, she grown up near her grand father from childhood.

She was born in Kudki and spent her childhood days in Merta. She was the greatest devote of lord Krishna.

When their people force ly married her to Bhojraj without her acceptance. As she was the devote of Krishna she never treated Bhojraj as her husband and given all her faith in Krishna.

After her husband death in a war. She was treated badly and their in-laws tried to kill her in many ways.

One day as they sent her a box with a cobra saying that a bouquet of flowers. When she opened it by thinking to take the flowers, the cobra was transformed into a beautiful of flowers and into a lord idol.

And the other day when they gave her poison saying that it was a nectar, it was also transformed into a prasad of lord Krishna.

As she keep much faith and love towards god, he was being saved by him in all the times.

CHAPTER THIRTEEN

UDDAVA

Since Uddava and Krishna are dearest friends from childhood.

After killing Kamsa Uddava came near Krishna to look into his wellness and Krishna told Uddava to go back to Vrindavan with a message to gopis who are waiting for Krishna's arrival.

And after the war of Krukshetra Uddava again came to Krishna to look into him. Then Krishna told Uddava to ask him for a wish whatever he wants to. Uddava told that he wants nothing the only thing he wants to know was the inner depth that he wasn't understood from Bhagavadgita which Krishna teaches to Arjuna.

Krishna smiles and asked him to tell his doubts and said ' Uddava what i was teaching you will called as Uddava gita.'

Then Uddava asked Krishna, what was the definition of a friend. The person who helps you in your bad days are called as friends, Krishna said. And Uddava started ' You are a true friend of pandavas. Why had you allowed the dice when it was going into wrong way which was turning by

Sakuni. Can't you stop it with your works? Can't you help your friends?' ' I was very fond of my friends and i was waiting outside for their call.

When Dharmaraj sat there to role the dice. Duryodana told them that Sakuni will roll the dice and i will stake my property. All the people accepted it. What happens if Dharmaraj said, my Krishna will role dice and i

will stake my property. Can you think who will win the game? And when the sat to play Dharmaraj told to himself that Krishna wouldn't be a part of this game. Then who am i to go there without their likeness?' Krishna replied.

' Why had you allowed the situation which they dragged Draupadi by pulling her hair hardly to game room? How can she bare it? Can't you think about her?' Uddava tears rolled down.

' When they taken Draupadi, she was busy in her preaching about her self. She din't even called me or thought about me. When they pulled her sari then she prayed for me to help, so i immediately went on to her and helped her in a second.' Krishna said.

' So, you only help your friends when they called you. Don't you help them if they din't thought about you?'

Krishna smiled shortly and said, ' Uddava, i was here to help Dharma. I won't interfere in any matters. I din't involve into any if some one din't called me. And that was the principle of God.'

' So, you are here just to watch our sins and wrong activities. Why are you not teaching and helping us when you stood behind us?'Uddava said. ' Uddava, your question itself had the answer. When i was your side, can't you think about me and go to right way thinking that lord stood next to us? Can't you thought about me in your tough times? Can't you believe in me?'

Uddava absorbed in bhakti. ' What a lofty truth' he praised.

Kamsa the king of Mathura.

Lord Vishnu took incarnation to kill Kamsa as he was troubling all the people in his kingdom. So Vishnu took incarnate as Krishna in Dwapara yuga.

Krishna waited for the turn to kill Kamsa when he was in Vrindavan. As he was growing older his sins count was being increased. Krishna became angry and beheaded him infront of his kingdom. And it was also called Kamsa Vadha.

Kamsa attempted many and many attempts to kill Krishna. Krishna came to Mathura to kill Kamsa with Balarama leaving Vrindavan.

CHAPTER FOURTEEN

KAMSA.

Kamsa the king of Mathura.

Lord Vishnu took incarnation to kill Kamsa as he was troubling all the people in his kingdom. So Vishnu took incarnate as Krishna in Dwapara yuga.

Kamsa learned that his sister Devaki was going to give birth to a baby boy who will be the reason for his death. From then he puts Vasudeva and devaki in jail and tortured them. Even though akasavani told him the eighth child will be the cause of his death, he killed all the seven kids who born to Devaki. And the eighth one was Krishna. Vaudeva saved him by crossing Yamuna and places him near Yashoda and Nanda.

Krishna waited for the turn to kill Kamsa when he was in Vrindavan. As he was growing older his sins count was being increased. Krishna became angry and beheaded him infront of his kingdom. And it was also called Kamsa Vadha.

Kamsa attempted many and many attempts to kill Krishna. Krishna came to Mathura to kill Kamsa with Balarama leaving Vrindavan.

One day they both went to a wrestlers competition. There they saw Chanura and Mushtika who was known as very popular wrestlers. They were sent there by Kamsa to kill Krishna. As per the plan, Chanura taunted Krishna very much to make fight with him. As Krishna was only a 16 year old boy. The crowd yelled saying it was not dharma. But Chanura pointed Krishna and continued taunted him. Then Krishna took his father's blessings and went onto the ring to fight with Chanura. On the other side Balarama too went in by Mushtika's calling. They both went on fight and finally Balarama killed Mushtika. And Chanura was killed by Krishna. Listening to their deaths Kamsa got anger and went to kill them by grouping many soldiers.

As Krishna was waiting to kill Kamsa he took the chance and killed him by beheading him in front of many people.

These are only few.

There were many people in Krishnas life who aided him in everystep.

Radha rani, Balaram, Yashoda, Vasudeva, Devaki, Nanda, Arjuna, Subhadra, Abhimanyu, Draupadi many and many more.

Hare Krishna.

www.ingramcontent.com/pod-product-compliance
Lightning Source LLC
Chambersburg PA
CBHW020655160726
47991CB00003B/1198